## Praise for *Doggy Loves Autumn*

Doggy Loves Autumn is as delicious as the first taste of home baked pumpkin pie. Ella is a beautiful dog and an enticing playmate. No child could resist following along as Ella romps through her favorite places, crunching through fallen leaves, tunneling through tall stands of hardy field flowers and watching her people family prepare for autumn holidays. Perfect for both pre-readers and emergent readers, the pictures give excellent clues for little ones to anticipate the accompanying text message. This will be a favorite "I wanna read this story again, please."

Pam Lemery Fitros, children's book author

A very sweet story. It gets the kids and the "kid in you" involved in Ella's life. I like that the author asks the children questions, so that they are involved in the story, and they're able to contribute to it. The use of actual photos instead of illustrations makes it very real, especially if the family reading this has a dog. I could see a child saying that their dog did some of the same things in the book. It's a book I'd read again. Great job!

Andrea Wingreen Muldoon

Doggie Loves Autumn pulls the child into learning with interactive questions. Fun and colorful pictures beautifully illustrate the concept on each page. Ella becomes a playmate for the child to enjoy the story. This could easily become a child's favorite book!

Majetta Morris

What a fun picture book about a beautiful, lovable, gentle dog named Ella. A good early reader for children to read themselves - or better yet for an adult to read to them. Questions posed on almost every page engage the child in a nice discussion about how the child also loves Autumn.  I suggest picking up "Doggy Finds Her Bone" and "Doggy's Busy Day" too!

Diane Howell Topkis

# *Wait!*

*Because we appreciate you as a reader,*
*please accept our gifts to you, which include...*

1.  **An email letting you know when Ella's next book will be offered FREE as a *Kindle* download**

2.  **FREE coloring pages of Ella**

3.  **An entry into the monthly drawing for a FREE *Ella The Doggy* book.  (Five winners will be selected).**

You will receive your download of the coloring pages immediately.  Winners for the books will be picked at the end of each month and notified by Email.  You need to go to www.ellathedoggy.com to register for the monthly drawing.  Names of the winners will be posted at the beginning of each month.

**Just visit the site below!**

**www.ellathedoggy.com!**

# Doggy Loves Autumn

Jayne Flaagan

Husky Publishing
East Grand Forks, MN
email: djflaagan@gra.midco.net

*"Doggy Loves Autumn "*
is dedicated to my Mother "In-Law"
Pat, who was a librarian, an
avid reader and an amazing person!

*Jayne lives in East Grand Forks, MN
with her husband and a silly dog
named (you guessed it!) Ella.
She also has three great kids!*

Ella the Doggy loves autumn!

Autumn is one of the four seasons.

Sometimes people use the word
"*fall*" instead of the word "*autumn.*"

Do you think it is because so
many leaves fall from the trees?

Ella's favorite time to take walks is in the fall.

What is your favorite season?

The weather is much cooler in
the fall than it is in the summer.

Ella does not get too warm from running
when she plays outside this time of year.

Sometimes this doggy has to wait for the people in her family to catch up with her.

She cannot speak to say "*hurry up please.*"

She just wags her tail very fast
and has to be patient.

In the fall season it is too cold for flowers
to keep growing in Ella's backyard...

but she found some beautiful yellow flowers on her walk!

What color of flower do you like?

In winter, the water in the river will
get so cold that it will freeze.

What is water called when it freezes?

Ella went to the playground one fall day,
but no children were playing there.

In the fall, all the kids go back to school.

Do you go to school to learn new things?

There was no one at the campground either.

In Minnesota where Ella lives, it is
too cold to sleep outside in the fall.

In autumn, it is also too cold for things to grow in the garden, but Ella found a big orange carrot there!

What vegetables do you eat?

Lots of pretty red apples were falling
from the apple tree in the back yard.

There are too many apples for Ella to count.

How high can you count?

Ella wanted to dress up as a princess
for a costume party in October...

but her crown kept falling off her head.

She tried on a "*Little Red Riding Hood*" costume next, but her ears were too big for the hood.

She did not mind, though.
She looked more like the wolf in that story anyway!

When trick-or-treaters came to the door for Halloween,
Ella saw children dressed up in all kinds of costumes.

Do you ever wear costumes?

Someone in the house made
cookies for a Halloween party.

What are the cookies shaped like?

What other shapes do you know?

Ella found even more pumpkins in another room.
They had funny faces carved in them.

Do you know what a pumpkin is
called when it looks like this?

You are right if you said, "jack-o-lantern!"

Thanksgiving is a holiday in November.

Ella watched a pie being made for that special day.

Do you have a favorite holiday?

Ella did not get to eat a slice of pie or have any cookies.

She got something that she liked even better.

What is she licking from the jar?

During the day, Ella likes to play outside in the leaves.

What does she do with the leaves at night time?

Yes, she makes a bed out of the leaves.

She is getting her rest so she can
play again tomorrow – just like you!

*Ella the Doggy*

Made in the USA
San Bernardino, CA
12 December 2014